Rivers Of Living Water

All About the Holy Spirit

Richard L. Madison

Cover design, entitled,
The Upper Room by: Judy Stacks
                    P.O. Box 25
                    Parrish, Alabama
                    (205) 686-7803

Layout by: Four Winds Publishing & Distribution
                 (706) 882-5368

Dedication

I want to thank my wonderful wife, Laura, for all her hard work on this project, and whom also saved my life in 1992 by donating one of her kidneys to me, and giving me two handsome boys. Thank-you honey for all your patience.

Special thanks to my mother, Jewel Kelley, also known as Pretty Red Wing, who is the Beloved Woman of the Cherokee Tribe of Northeast Alabama. Thank-you for my Indian name, Spirit Walker. Thank-you for all your love and support throughout the years.

Acknowledgments

Special thanks to Religious Products Company in Mableton, GA, for supplying our ministry with audio supplies. 1-800-241-8096.

I would also like to thank Tom and Mary Ann Root for their love, prayers, and support.

Special thanks to Barbara Jones for her love, prayers, and support to Operation Healing Ministry.

Contents

Chapter One

Have Ye Received The Holy Ghost Since Ye Believed?

The Great Commission

" *And he said unto them, Go ye into all the world, and preach the gospel to every creature. He that believeth and is baptized shall be saved; but he that believeth not shall be damned"* (Mark 16:15,16). John the Baptist was fulfilling the prophecy of Malachi when he began baptizing in the river Jordan. He was a voice in the wilderness declaring that people must repent and be baptized for the kingdom of heaven was at hand. *"Behold, I will send my messenger, and he shall prepare the way before me: and the Lord, whom ye seek, shall suddenly come to his temple, even the messenger of the covenant, whom ye delight in: behold, he shall come, saith the LORD of hosts"* (Malachi 3:1). John was the messenger sent ahead of the Messiah. He was to proclaim that the Messiah was here to remove the sin of the world. John said he was sent to bear witness of the

7

Redeemer. John was baptizing the people in natural water, but the Messiah would baptize them in the Holy Ghost and fire. *"I indeed baptize you with water unto repentance: but he that cometh after me is mightier than I, whose shoes I am not worthy to bear: he shall baptize you with the Holy Ghost, and with fire"* (Matthew 3:11). John the Baptist was getting people's hearts ready to receive from the living God. John declared Jesus as the Lamb of God. After John baptized Jesus in water, the Holy Ghost came upon Jesus without measure. *"Then cometh Jesus from Galilee to Jordan unto John, to be baptized of him. And Jesus when he was baptized, went up straightway out of the water: and, lo, the heavens were opened unto him, and he saw the Spirit of God descending like a dove, and lighting upon him: And lo a voice from heaven, saying, This is my beloved Son, in whom I am well pleased"* (Matthew 3:13,16,17). Jesus was about thirty years of age according to Luke 3:23. Jesus was now starting His public ministry. Numbers chapter four said that all who were called into the ministry must be between thirty to fifty years of age. Jesus once again was fulfilling the Law. He was about to make it possible for you and I to receive the Holy Spirit and become a royal priest-hood. Jesus did not have to repent when He was baptized because He never sinned. He was a perfect spotless lamb. But before you and I get water baptized or filled with the Holy Spirit we must repent. We must ask Jesus to forgive us, and come into our heart. God then washes away our past. *"And their sins and iniquities will I remember no more"* (Hebrews 10:17). *"That if thou shalt confess with thy mouth the Lord Jesus, and shalt believe in thine heart that God hath raised him from the dead, thou shalt be saved"* (Romans 10:9). In order to declare the great commission, we must first be partakers of the great commission. God chose the preaching of the gospel to save souls. The world does not understand what the church is all about.

The gospel of Jesus Christ is a simple message. God sent His only begotten son to die on a cross to redeem mankind from wickedness. We can overcome the lust of the eye, the lust of the flesh and the pride of life through faith in the shed blood of Jesus. When we are born again, God's Spirit comes to live in us. God has commanded for us to be water baptized after we repent. It is not the water that saves us, but it is showing obedience to the gospel. It shows the Lord that we wish to please Him. It is part of out testimony that we have a clean conscience and we are new creatures. ***"Go ye therefore, and teach all nations, baptizing them in the name of the Father, and of the Son, and of the Holy Ghost: Teaching them to observe all things whatsoever I have commanded you: and, lo, I am with you always, even unto the end of the world"*** (Matthew 28:19,20). ***"Then Peter said unto them, Repent, and be baptized every one of you in the name of Jesus Christ for the remission of sins, and ye shall receive the gift of the Holy Ghost"*** (Acts 2:38). We must obey the Word of God if we expect the benefits and promises from the Word of God. Jesus has given us authority to baptize other believers in water. We should help them become disciples to carry out the great commission. God wants to use all of us to spread the gospel and evangelize the world. Jesus Christ came and died and arose from the dead for you and I. He made it possible for us to be delivered from the curse of the law and the sin of the world. Jesus came to destroy the works of the devil. Before Jesus came, the Holy Spirit only came upon four groups of people such as the kings, priests, prophets, and judges. But since the death, burial, resurrection, and accession of Jesus, the Holy Spirit now comes to abide within all of us that are saved. *"For by one Spirit are we all baptized into one body"* (I Corinthians 12:13a). *"And I will pray the Father, and he shall give you another Comforter, that he may abide with you for ever; Even the Spirit of truth; whom the world cannot receive, because it seeth him not, neither knoweth him: but ye know him; for he dwelleth with you, and shall be in you"* (John 14:16,17). To be water baptized is to acknowledge the great commission. We first believe and then we are baptized. The word baptize comes from the Greek word *baptidzo*, from *bapto*, which means to dip, to bury, or to cover. Also to surround or submerge. Here are some examples: *"And Jesus, when he was baptized, went up straightway out of the water"* (Matthew 3:16); *"And John also was baptizing in Aenon near to Salim, because there was much water there"* (John 3:23); *"how that all our fathers were under the cloud, and all passed through the sea; And were all baptized unto Moses in the cloud and in the sea"* (1 Corinthians 10:1,2); *"For as many of you as have been baptized into Christ have put on Christ"* (Galatians 3:27); *"Buried with him in baptism, wherein also ye are risen with him through the faith of the operation of God"* (Colossians 2:12).

Holy Spirit Baptism

"And, being assembled together with them, commanded them that they should not depart from Jerusalem, but wait for the promise of the Father, which, saith He, ye have heard of me. For John truly baptized with water; but ye

shall be baptized with the Holy Ghost not many days hence" (Acts 1:4, 5). Jesus told His disciples they were going to be baptized or saturated in the Holy Spirit. We need the witness of the glory cloud in our life. Jesus referred to the baptism of the Holy Spirit as a promise from the Father. Jesus told His disciples to wait for the promise of the Father. *"And, behold, I send the promise of my Father upon you: but tarry ye in the city of Jerusalem, until ye be endued with power from on high"* (Luke 24:49). Jesus told His disciples that they would receive authority and boldness when they were filled with the Holy Ghost. *"But ye shall receive power, after that the Holy Ghost is come upon you; and ye shall be witnesses unto me both in Jerusalem, and in all Judea, and in Samaria, and unto the uttermost part of the earth "* (Acts 1:8). The Greek word for power in this verse is **_dunamis_**. The word dynamite is derived from **_dunamis._** When a person is born again or receives Jesus Christ into their heart, the Spirit of God enters into them. Jesus comes into our life and heart by His Spirit. God never reminds us of our past. We can live for God in peace, holiness, and righteousness because of the Holy Spirit. The Spirit of God will convict us of sin. If we do something wrong, we must ask for forgiveness, and make things right. In order to fulfill all righteousness, we also need to be baptized in water. Jesus also wants us to be filled with the Holy Ghost. As disciples of Christ we need the full infilling of the Holy Spirit. We must ask the Lord to fill us and we must then believe that He will. The writer of Hebrews mentions the doctrine of <u>baptisms</u>. *"Of the doctrine of baptisms, and of laying on of hands"* (Hebrews 6:2). The word baptism in this scripture is plural. The apostle Paul found certain disciples of John the Baptist in Ephesus and ask them had they been filled with the Holy Ghost. *"He said unto them, Have*

11

ye received the Holy Ghost since ye believed?" (Acts 19:2). They had not heard of Jesus' death, burial, and resurrection, therefore, they could not have been born again nor received the Holy Spirit. They had only been baptized in water after the manner of John's preaching. Paul told them that John the Baptist was the fore-runner for Jesus and that everyone must believe on Christ Jesus. Paul explained how Christ came to take away the sins of the world. *"When they heard this they were baptized in the name of the Lord Jesus. And when Paul laid his hands upon them, the Holy Ghost came on them; and they spake with tongues, and prophesied"* (Acts 19:5,6). These men were baptized in water, and then, they were baptized in the Holy Ghost. Biblical evidence of being filled or baptized in the Holy Ghost is to speak in other tongues, and to prophesy. This same experience is also recorded on the day of Pentecost in Acts chapter 2. According to Acts 1:5 about 120 people had gone to the upper room in Jerusalem to wait on the promise Jesus had mentioned. Perhaps they were not sure what was going to happen, but they were being obedient to Christ's command to go and tarry until they be endued with power from on high. They appointed another disciple to take Judas Iscariot's place. They then went to the upper room for seven days praying and speaking of the things concerning Christ. The Feast of Pentecost arrived for the people to celebrate in the streets. They were preparing sacrifices according Leviticus 23:16-22. However, the 120 people in the upper room had received Jesus as their Savior. He had become their sacrifice. They were expecting something spiritual and powerful to happen. They waited on God. *"And when the day of Pentecost was fully come, they were all with one accord in one place. And suddenly there came a sound from heaven as of a rushing mighty wind, and* *it filled the house where they were sitting. And there appeared unto them cloven tongues like as of fire, and it sat upon each of them. And <u>they were all filled with the Holy Ghost, and began to speak with other tongues</u>, as the Spirit gave them utterance*" (Acts 2:1-4). God wants every born-again Christian to have this experience. This is called the infilling or baptism of the Holy Spirit. The Lord wants to lead us and guide us by His Spirit. The Holy Spirit is the teacher and He wants to teach us many things. The Word of God is revealed to us by the Holy Spirit. Have you been born-again? If so, have you been baptized in water and in the Holy Ghost? Have you ever spoken in other tongues? What a wonderful gift this is to receive from God. There are some people who get born-again, sanctified, and filled with the Holy Ghost all at one time. Others though, may have a progressive work of Grace to take place in their lives. God knows our hearts and He understands what we need before we even ask Him. If we hunger and thirst for more of God, then we will receive more of Him. The 120 people in the upper room that received the baptism of the Holy Ghost tarried and hungered for more of Jesus. These people would not have received the fullness of the Holy Ghost if they had not tarried, prayed, and believed. They wanted more. They were not satisfied with Jesus breathing on them once. They wanted another breath Praise God! *"And when he had said this, he breathed on them, and saith unto them, Receive ye the Holy Ghost*" (John 20:22). The disciples met Jesus after His resurrection. They believed on Him as their Savior. At this time they became born-again. No one was actually born again until Jesus died and then rose again. Jesus breathed on the disciples and the Holy Spirit entered into them. However, they were not filled or baptized in the Holy Ghost until the day of Pentecost.

This was seven days after Jesus' ascension. The day of Pentecost is fifty days after the feast of Passover (Leviticus 23:5,16). Jesus died at Passover. He was dead for three days and three nights. According to Acts 1:3 Jesus preached for forty days after His resurrection. Add forty days to the three days He was dead and this equals forty-three days. Pentecost in the Greek means fifty. Forty-three days from fifty days leaves seven. Seven days after Jesus ascended up into the clouds the Holy Ghost was poured out upon the 120 in the upper room.

Drunk In The Spirit

"And he saith unto them, ye shall drink indeed of my cup and be baptized with the baptism that I am baptized with" (Matthew 20:23). The apostle Paul said, *"And be not drunk with wine, wherein is excess; but be filled with the Spirit"* (Ephesians 5:18). Praying in the Spirit makes us strong. *"But ye, beloved, building up yourselves on your most holy faith, praying in the Holy Ghost"* (Jude v.20). Jesus said in Matthew 7:11 *"If ye then, being evil, know how to give good gifts unto your children, how much more shall your Father which is in heaven give good things to them that ask him"*. Ask the Lord to baptize you in the Holy Ghost. Jesus said, *"And I will pray the Father, and he shall give you another comforter, that he may abide with you for ever"* (John 14:16). Jesus said we could drink from His cup or have what he had. We can have the same baptism he received. If we are filled with the Holy Spirit, some people may think we are drunk or intoxicated with alcohol. When we are filled with the Spirit, we may have characteristics or symptoms similar to one drunk on alcohol. The 120 people in the upper room on the Feast of Pentecost were

accused of being drunk on alcohol because they were speaking in other languages. *"Cretes, and Arabians, we do hear them speak in our tongues the wonderful works of God. And they were all amazed, and were in doubt, saying one to another, what meaneth this? Other mocking said, "These men are full of new wine"* (Acts 2:11-13). People are still full of doubt in our day and time. People still mock and criticize because they do not understand the anointing of God. Don't doubt this wonderful gift of the baptism of the Holy Ghost. Receive this gift and be blessed. These 120 that were filled with the Spirit spoke in a language they had never studied, yet they glorified God. Perhaps they staggered, laughed, jumped, run and even rolled. I believe it was a prophetic statement when those mocking said these are full of new wine. They were not filled with the wine of the world, but with the Holy Ghost. Peter stood up after hearing the doubt and unbelief and said these people were not drunk as they had presumed, especially since it was only 9:00 a.m. But this was fulfilling the prophecy of Joel. *"For these are not drunken, as ye suppose, seeing it is but the third hour of the day. But this that which is spoken by the prophet Joel; AND IT SHALL COME TO PASS IN THE LAST DAYS, SAITH GOD, I WILL POUR OUT OF MY SPIRIT UPON ALL FLESH: AND YOUR SONS AND YOU DAUGHTERS SHALL PROPHESY, AND YOUR YOUNG MEN SHALL SEE VISIONS, AND YOUR OLD MEN SHALL DREAM DREAMS: AND ON MY SERVANTS AND ON MY HANDMAIDENS I WILL POUR OUT IN THOSE DAYS OF MY SPIRIT; AND THEY SHALL PROPHESY"* (Acts 2:15-18). We are seeing more people get filled with the Holy Spirit right now than ever before. God is revealing Himself to multitudes of people who want more of Him. People are tired of just going to church and sitting on a pew and hearing a dead sermon. People are now driving, flying, even walking, or whatever it takes to get in the presence of the Lord. God wants us to have the fullness of His Spirit to guide us into all truth. *"Even the Spirit of Truth; whom the world cannot receive, because it seeth Him not, neither knoweth Him: but ye know Him; for He dwelleth with you, and shall be in you"* (John 14:17). The world walks by sight. The people of God walk by faith. We are saved by faith. We are filled with the Holy Spirit by faith. We are healed by faith, The just shall live by faith. *"For therein is the righteousness of God revealed from faith to faith: as it is written, THE JUST SHALL LIVE BY FAITH"* (Romans 1:17). Jesus is pouring out His Spirit on all flesh world wide. He is raising up sons and daughters to fulfill His will. We are to proclaim the gospel of Jesus Christ. We will preach, teach, and live the whole Bible.

True Worshippers

God is raising up true worshippers to worship Him in spirit and in truth. *"But the hour cometh and now is, when the true worshippers shall worship the Father in spirit and in truth: for the Father seeketh such to worship Him. God is a Spirit: and they that worship Him must worship Him in spirit and in truth"* (John 4:23,24). We need to be filled with the spirit in order to worship in spirit. When we are baptized in the spirit, we can pray in the spirit. We edify ourselves and build up ourselves by praying in the spirit. If we are believers we will pray in the spirit. *"And these signs shall follow them that believe; In my name shall they cast out devils; they shall speak with new tongues"* (Mark 16:17). A lady once told me that she did not believe in miracles, healings, and speaking in tongues. I told her this is why these signs did not follow or accompany her. We must believe to receive. If we doubt, we will do without. Many churches, now teach that the baptism of the Holy Spirit left the earth or stopped existing when the Bible was wrote or when the last disciples died, but this is not true. Speaking in other tongues is also a sign to the unbeliever. *"Wherefore tongues are for a sign, not to them that believe, but to them that believe not"* (I Corinthians 14:22). Paul said God has established the church with apostles, prophets, teachers, miracles, gifts of healings, helps, governments, and divers kinds of tongues (I Corinthians 12:28). Apostles could not be done away with because the church is still here. And last but not least, Paul says we have divers, or different kinds of tongues, for the body of Christ. After Jesus was raised from the dead he gave gifts to the church. *"Wherefore he saith, WHEN HE ASCENDED UP ON HIGH, HE LED CAPTIVITY CAPTIVE, AND GAVE GIFTS UNTO MEN. And he gave some, apostles, and some, prophets; and some, evangelist; and some, pastors and teachers; for the perfecting of the saints, for the work of the ministry, for the edifying of the body of Christ"* (Ephesians 4:8, 11, 12). Well, we the saints still need perfecting. This five fold ministry is still here today because the church has not been caught up, or raptured yet. I believe that the non-Pentecostal churches have good people in them. We are all family in Christ that preach and teach that salvation is received because Jesus shed His blood for us. We confess with our mouth and believe in our heart and live a Godly and holy life. However, some of our brothers and sisters in the Lord are living beneath their privileges. Anything that comes from God is good. The nine gifts of the Holy Spirit in I Corinthians 12 (which we will cover later) are in operation today. They are in operation as the Holy Spirit moves about among believers. We can not operate the gifts whenever we want, but we can make ourselves available and wait upon the Lord. If we are walking in the Spirit we are not fulfilling the desires of the flesh. We that are spiritually minded have life and peace. To disregard the gifts of God and the working of the Holy Spirit is to be carnally minded. *"For to be carnally minded is death; but to be spiritually minded is life and peace. Because the carnal mind is enmity against God: so then they that are in the flesh can not please God"* (Romans 8:6-8). The natural mind can not receive the spiritual things of God. We must crucify the body and make it subject to the will of God.

We must come out from among the world and be a different person than the world knew us as. We must walk in peace and holiness to see God. *"Follow peace with all men, and holiness, without which no man shall see the Lord"* (Hebrews 12:14). We can never see God in His purest form while we are in the flesh. This is why we will be changed at his appearing. But we can see the Lord working through us and others. We can be used by the Holy Spirit to help others. We can also allow the Holy Spirit to pray out of us the divine will of God. We can be healed by praying in the Spirit. *"Likewise the Spirit also helpeth our infirmities: for we know not what we should pray for as we ought: but the Spirit itself maketh intercession for us with groanings which cannot be uttered. And he that searcheth the hearts knoweth what is the mind of the Spirit, because he maketh intercession for the saints according to the will of God"* (Romans 8:26,27). Paul tells us that God prays through us by His Spirit. He knows what we need before we even ask.

18

He wants to touch us. He desires to heal our hearts, and broken spirits. He will remove our hurts and our pains. He loves us. He has made it possible for us to speak His language. Though we don't understand many times what we are saying when we are praying in other tongues, the scripture tells us that we are speaking mysteries to God, and we are edifying ourselves. *"For he that speaketh in an unknown tongue speaketh not unto men, but unto God: for no man understandeth him; howbeit in the Spirit he speaketh mysteries. He that speaketh in an unknown tongue edifieth himself. Wherefore let him that speaketh in an unknown tongue pray that he might interpret. For if I pray in an unknown tongue, my Spirit prayeth, by my understanding is unfruitful. What is it then? I will pray with the Spirit, and I will pray with the understanding also: I will sing with the Spirit, and I will sing with the understanding also"* (I Corinthians 14:2, 4, 13-15). If we are walking in the Spirit, it should not be a problem for us to pray in the Spirit. We should also pray for the revelation or understanding of what we are praying about. I pray in the Spirit many times while I am driving, flying, or doing chores around home. You don't have to be at a church building to seek the Lord. In Fact, we are the temple of the Holy Ghost. *"What? know ye not that your body is the temple of the Holy Ghost which is in you"* (I Corinthians 6:19). Jesus fellowships with us by His Spirit. I receive the understanding of what I am praying about many times while I am praying. There are times I see missionaries, or people in need. I have seen relatives in the Spirit and I realized I was praying for them. I pray in the Spirit if I am discouraged, or if I feel that I've been let down by others. Immediately I am picked up by the Holy Spirit. We can encourage ourselves. Most of the body of Christ has not learned how to encourage themselves. If you ever sing in the Spirit you will see how much it blesses and lifts you up. I love to just trust God and start singing in the Spirit. It takes faith to pray or sing in a language you have never studied. This kind of faith also pleases God. You just have to believe that God understands you and that you are progressing in the kingdom of God. You must press through, kick down the gates of hell, and proceed into the deep things of God. The deep calleth unto the deep. When you pray in the Spirit, you are allowing God to ask himself to do something for you. *"For now we see through a glass, darkly; but then face to face: now I know in part; but then shall I know even as also I am known* "(I Corinthians 13:12).

Praise God, one day we will be with Jesus in a glorified body. We have a mansion waiting on us. We are going to heaven very soon. God has given us tools to help us get there. A man ask me one time if he would go to heaven without the Holy Ghost. I told him I did not want to go to the store or drive down the road without the Holy Ghost. The Holy Ghost comes into us when we are saved. So in reality a person cannot go to heaven without the Holy Spirit. A person can go to heaven without the baptism of the Holy Spirit. However, they will miss out on so many wonderful experiences.

Divers Kind of Tongues

We have the Bible, the armor of God, and we are covered in the precious blood of Jesus. We have power in our words, and we can have the gift of the Holy Ghost with the evidence of praying in other tongues. When the 120 people in the upper room received the Holy Spirit, the Bible reveals in Acts 2:9-11 that over fifteen

20

different nationalities were present. They heard 120 people speaking in their languages. In I Corinthians 14:2, Paul speaks about an unknown tongue. God has a pure language that man can not learn in any college or school. It has been said that there are thousands of different languages and dialects in the world. When we are baptized in the Holy Spirit, we may speak in the languages of men, or, we may speak in that unknown language, God's language. In Genesis 1:3 God said let there be light. But what language did He speak it in? We think that He spoke it in English because our Bible is written in English. The Russians think He spoke it in their language because their Bible is translated in Russian. The Spanish think He spoke it in their language, and so on. But I believe that God spoke it in a creative language, a tongue not known to man. When we pray in the Holy Spirit, we are allowing God to speak through us in that creative language once again. The Old Testament was written in Hebrew. The New Testament was written in Greek. The King James Version of the Bible was put together in 1611 A.D. No matter what language the Word of God is printed in, it will never change, nor will it ever fail. We must study the Word of God to know the voice of God. Jesus said my sheep know my voice. Whatever God says to you, it will line up with the written Word of God, the Bible. The Holy Spirit will always reveal the written Word of God to us. He is our teacher and instructor in all righteousness. Many people have been born-again, but they do not have the power of God, nor the gifts of the Spirit in operation in their lives, or in their churches. The greatest gift from God is to be born-again, but don't get satisfied with salvation only. There is so much more that God wants to give you. Seek Him and ask Him to fill you with His Holy Spirit and to use the gifts of the Spirit in your life. *"Ask, and it shall be given you; seek, and ye shall find; knock, and it shall be opened to you: For everyone that asketh receiveth; and he that seeketh findeth; and to him that knocketh it shall be opened*" (Matthew 7:7-8). It is the Father's good pleasure to give unto us the kingdom. He wants us to get in the river. If we will get in the river, the river will get into us. *"He that believeth on me, as the scripture hath said, out of his belly shall flow rivers of living water. But this spake he of the Spirit, which they that believe on Him should receive*" (John 17:38, 39).

In Acts 2:38, 39 *"Peter said unto them, repent, and be baptized every one of you in the name of Jesus Christ for the remission of sins, and ye shall receive the gift of the Holy Ghost. For the promise is unto you, and to your children, and to all that are afar off, even as many as the Lord our God shall call*". When we do what God says to do, and become obedient, God pours His Spirit out. He is no respector of persons. What he does for one, he will do for another. Luke said in Acts 3:19 *"Repent ye therefore, and be converted, that your sins may be blotted out, when the times of refreshing shall come from the presence of the Lord*". We will always get refreshed when we come before the Lord humble, confessing our sins. Our strength comes from the Lord. We acknowledge Him, and give Him all praise, and He will comfort us. The Spirit of God was not just for the 27 apostles in the early church days. He is for all of us. We receive the Holy Spirit when we are born-again, but we may not receive the **fullness** of the Holy Ghost. Notice that in Acts chapter 8 verses 5-8 Philip the evangelist went to the city of Samaria and preached Christ unto the people. They heard and saw the miracles that God worked though Philip. Many people were healed from diseases and delivered from devils.

Multitudes were born-again as they believed on Jesus Christ. However, they did not receive all that God had for them. They had not received the Holy Ghost baptism yet. But Acts 8:14-17 reveals how they got filled. *"Now when the apostles which were at Jerusalem heard that Samaria had received the Word of God, they sent unto them Peter and John: Who, when they were come down, prayed for them, that they might receive the Holy ghost: (for as yet he was fallen upon none of them: only they were baptized in the name of the Lord Jesus.) Then laid they their hands on them, and they received the Holy Ghost"*. God poured His Spirit out on the Samaritans, whom the Jews thought very little of. But God is no respector of persons. The Samaritans received salvation and were water baptized, and then they were filled with the Holy Spirit. Now scripture reveals that a person can receive the Holy Ghost baptism before they are water baptized. However before a person is water baptized or Holy Ghost baptized they must first have received salvation. Peter witnessed Gentiles getting baptized in the Holy Ghost with the evidence of speaking in other tongues. *"While Peter yet spake these words, the Holy Ghost fell on all them which heard the word. And they of the circumcision which believed were astonished, as many as came with Peter, because that the Gentiles also was poured out the gift of the Holy Ghost. For they heard them speak with other tongues, and magnify God. Then answered Peter, can any man forbid water, that these should not be baptized, which have received the Holy Ghost as well as we? And he commanded them to be baptized in the name of the Lord "*(Acts 10:44-48). How did Peter know that the gift of the Holy Ghost, or baptism of the Holy Ghost

23

had been poured out on the Gentiles? Because he heard them speak in other tongues. They spoke words that he did not understand nor did they. After they had believed on Christ Jesus and were born-again, they were filled with the Holy Ghost. Then they were water baptized. So this reveals that God can, and will pour His Spirit out on all flesh, and the only condition that has to be met, is for them to be born-again first.

A Promise of Power

God is not a racist, He is not poor, or worried, or sick, or weak, and He does not want us to be either. He gives us His Spirit to help us be comforted, guided, strengthened, and to walk in righteousness. The more we acknowledge the Holy Spirit and allow him to use us, the more effective we are as a witness for Him. We can do nothing on our own. We need the anointing of the Holy Spirit. He gives us love, power and a sound mind. No wonder Jesus said "*Ye shall receive power after that the Holy Ghost is come upon you*" (Acts 1:8a). Jesus spoke of the infilling, or baptism of the Holy Ghost as a promise. "*But wait for the promise of the Father, which, saith he, ye have heard of me. For John truly baptized with water; but ye shall be baptized with the Holy Ghost not many days hence*" (Acts 1:4, 5). "*And behold, I send the promise of my Father upon you: but tarry ye in the city of Jerusalem, until ye be endued with power from on high*" (Luke 24:49). The baptism of the Holy Ghost is definitely a promise of power. Do you have this power in your life? The enemy knows if you have the power of God and the gift of the Holy Ghost. The enemy I'm speaking of, is Satan and the one-third of the angles who were kicked out of heaven. The devil knows if you are avoiding him. He knows if

24

you are weak and intimidated by his forces of evil. He also knows what will happen if you begin to seek more of Jesus. He knows the authority that every born-again Christian should have. This is why he fights the full gospel message. He does not want you and I to have a Pentecostal experience. He wants people to be afraid and shy. Satan does not want you to receive boldness. He has deceived millions of religious people, and even born-again Christians, with the traditions of men. Multitudes have joined a church and have not even been born-again. Many people are proud of their denomination because their family has always been a part of that faith or a member of that certain church. Yet their church leaders will denounce the power of God and the baptism of the Holy Ghost. We should expect that from the non-believers and cults who denounce Jesus as the Son of God. But from born-again Christians who proclaim Jesus as their Lord and Savior, this is blasphemy. Take this note of caution: If a person speaks negative or evil of the Lord or Holy Ghost get away from them. You can witness to them but don't hang around them all the time. If they are your spouse or family member, then pray for them, and win them to Jesus with your faithfulness. The unbelieving spouse is sanctified, or drawn, by the Spirit of God towards repentance through the believer. You may be the only "Bible" someone ever sees. As we draw close to God, He draws close to us. A person must be drawn by the Spirit of God in order to be saved. Jesus draws people to himself through us the believer. We preach the gospel with our testimony and the life we live. So as I was giving caution to the wise, if you don't know anything about the Holy Ghost, then don't say anything bad about Him, or the people who are in His presence. *"Verily I say unto you, all sins shall be forgiven unto the sons of men, and blasphemies wherewith soever they shall blaspheme: But he that shall blaspheme against the Holy Ghost hath never forgiveness, but is in danger of eternal damnation*" (Mark 3:29). God is a Spirit. He does not perform mighty deeds by His might or power, but by His Spirit. (Zechariah 4:6). When a person speaks evil of the Holy Spirit or denies His presence, they are speaking evil of God. Satan is wise and he causes many to be defiled by blasphemy. John said in 1 John 5:7 "*there are three that bear record in heaven, the Father, the Word, and the Holy Ghost: and these three are one.*" To speak evil of one of the manifestations of the God head is to speak evil of all three. The apostle Paul warns us in this manner, "***Let no corrupt communication proceed out of your mouth, but that which is good to the use of edifying, that it may minister grace unto the hearers. And grieve not the Holy Spirit of God, whereby ye are sealed unto the day of redemption***" (Ephesians 4:29, 30). Don't be deceived by Satan anymore, or by those who speak in vain, that God can not, or will not, do what He has done before. Jesus Christ is the same yesterday, and today, and forever (Hebrews 13:8). Since God has promised to pour His Spirit out on all flesh in these last days, it will happen. There is a great shaking taking place in the earth now. Whatever is false will fade away. That which is true will stand forever. Every good promise in the Bible is for you. There are thousands of promises in the Bible that belongs to the believer. We must know what they are to obtain them. Jesus gave us a new covenant with better promises. "***But now hath he obtained a more excellent ministry, by how much also he is the mediator of a better covenant, which was established upon better promises***" (Hebrews 8:6).

26

The Word of Truth

We must have a personal relationship with Jesus. The Holy Spirit will reveal Him to us. The Spirit of God is the teacher. He will feed us the "meat" of the Word of God. The "milk" of the Word is for the babes in Christ. The "meat" of the Word is for strength to the army of the Lord. The Word of God is a sure word of prophecy. If you don't believe it is just as real today as it was in the early church days, either you have been deceived, or you are not hungry for more of God. The apostle Paul told the Galatians that he marveled that they were troubled by some who would pervert the gospel of Christ by getting away from the full message. He said if he, or an angel from heaven, preach any other gospel unto them (which also pertain to us) than which has been preached, let him be accursed. (Galatians 1:6-9). John the revelator said, *"And if any man shall take away from the words of the book of this prophecy, God shall take away his part out of the book of life, and out of the holy city, and from the things which are written in this book"* (Revelation 22:19). Let us eat the whole book and be filled. I pray you get filled with the Spirit and begin *"Speaking to yourselves in Psalms and hymns and spiritual songs, singing and making melody in your heart to the Lord"* (Ephesians 5:19). We should be *"praying always with prayer and supplication in the Spirit, and watching there-unto with all perseverance and supplication for all saints"* (Ephesians 6:18). You can have this experience of singing in the Spirit. You can be happy. You can have as much of Jesus as you want. We are God's creation. He wants us to have life and to have it more abundantly. Don't get saved and satisfied. Get saved and sanctified, and filled with the Holy Ghost and fire. Christianity should not be stale and old. Religions of the world

27

are what is stale and dead. Jesus is not the God of the dead, He is the God of the living. If we are filled with the joy of the Lord we will raise holy hands without doubt and wrath. The joy of the Lord, is our strength. When I got filled with the Holy Ghost, I got filled with joy, faith, boldness and love. This is what everyone needs, but because of doubt and unbelief, many stagger around in fear, worry, and disappointment. Many people appear to be content and happy, but in reality, there is a void on the inside. Pride will stop them from receiving. While God is trying to birth a newness in them, Satan is telling them to worry about what others will think of them. Christ humbled Himself and became obedient even unto death. We must die out to this world in order to live. I said earlier that Satan knows if we have the power of God in our lives. God also knows where we stand with Him. People can deceive one another, but God is not deceived. *"Now if any man have not the Spirit of Christ, he is none of His. And if Christ be in you, the body is dead because of sin; but the Spirit is life because of righteousness. The Spirit itself beareth witness with our Spirit, that we are the children of God"* (Romans 8:9, 10, 16). We can know that we belong to God. We will bear good fruit. Our deeds will follow us. We will destroy the works of the devil with love. I use to want to get even with my enemies. Now I want to pray for them. We overcome evil with good. If God be for us, who can be against us. We are on the winning side. We that are called, chosen and elected are ordained to do the works of God. We are anointed and gifted. God will not take His gifts back. The gifts and callings of God are without repentance. God is with us. He will not let our words fall to the ground. Allow the vision of God to be birthed within you. *"Where there is no vision, the people perish"* (Proverbs 29:19). Let the Father anoint you as He anointed Jesus. It is the same Holy Spirit. *"There is one body, and one Spirit, even as ye are called in one hope of your calling; One Lord, one faith, one baptism, One God and Father of all, who is above all, and through all, and in you all"* (Ephesians 4:4-6). We all are a part of the body of Christ. Jesus is the head of this body. Though there be many members in the body, there is only one head. This is Jesus. We are His body. There is only one Holy Ghost. When we are born-again we receive the Spirit of God, this is how we become new creatures. Jesus comes to live in us by His Spirit, He is the only way to eternal life. There is no other faith or religion that can get us to heaven. Jesus said He was the only way. *"I am the way, the truth, and the life: no man cometh unto the Father, but by me"* (John 14:6). It is God's will for everyone to go to heaven, but in reality, we know that everyone will not. We have the opportunity to receive Jesus into our heart. If we refuse or neglect to do so and die without Jesus, we will spend eternity in a lake of fire. It will be a point of no return. It will be torment forever and ever. If we repent we can receive an anointing. This anointing justifies us to work for the Master in His Vineyard. We must work quickly. Multitudes shall be cast into outer darkness and torment because they don't love the truth.

"And with all deceivableness of righteousness in them that perish; because they received not the love of the truth, that they might be saved. And for this cause God shall send them strong delusion, that they should believe a lie: That they all might be damned who believed not the truth, but had pleasure in unrighteousness" (II Thessalonians 2:10-12).

What Jesus Came To Do

Jesus was anointed to do a work in His day and time. *"How God anointed Jesus of Nazareth with the Holy Ghost and with power: who went about doing good, and healing all that were oppressed of the devil; for God was with Him"* (Acts 10:38). Jesus was thirty years of age when He received the Holy Ghost without measure. His public ministry was approximately 3 1/2 years. He was crucified and raised from the dead. He ascended back to heaven to receive the glory He had left in the beginning. However, he said that He was coming back. *"I will not leave you comfortless: I will come to you"* (John 14:18). Not only does Jesus come to abide, or live, in us by His Spirit, but He is coming back to meet us in the air one day according to 1 Thessalonians 4:16, 17. We shall see Him as He is and be just like Him. We will receive a new body that will never get sick or tired. We will receive rewards for our labor. A robe, and a crown is waiting on us. Jesus has also prepared a place for us. *"In my Father's house are many mansions: if it were not so, I would have told you. I go to prepare a place for you. And if I go and prepare a place for you, I will come again and receive you unto myself; that where I am, there ye may be also"* (John 14:2,3). We should not worry about when or how this will happen, but rejoice and be glad because it will happen. We will be kings and priests unto God. For 1,000 years we will rule and reign with Christ in the Millennial Reign. John the revelator said that he saw a new city coming down, New Jerusalem, prepared as a bride adorned for her husband. As John saw these things in Revelation chapters 20 and 21 he was carried away in the Spirit to a great and high mountain. Let's allow God to carry us to a high place in Him by His Spirit. Who knows what He will show us. He will show us many things by His Spirit. The apostle Paul was caught up into the third heaven, even unto paradise. He heard unspeakable words, which was not lawful for a man to utter. *"I knew a man in Christ above fourteen years ago, (whether in the body, I cannot tell; or whether out of the body, I cannot tell: God knoweth;) such an one caught up to the third heaven. How that he was caught up into paradise, and heard unspeakable words, which it is not lawful for a man to utter"* (II Corinthians 12:2,4). Paul was not saying that this experience was against the law, but that this is impossible unless you are in the Spirit. Many people will quote I Corinthians 2:9 which says *"But as it is written, Eye hath not seen, nor ear heard, neither have entered into the heart of men, the things which God heth prepared for them that love Him."* But many people do not notice the very next scripture. *"But God hath revealed them unto us by His Spirit"* (I Corinthians 2:10). Paul went on to say no one knows or understand the things about God except the Spirit of God.

So if we are to learn of God we must get in tune with His Spirit. The spiritual concepts and laws that are in force and motion are foolish to the natural man. Our carnal mind can not conceive God or the ways of God. However, revelation knowledge belongs to the believer. God's ways and thoughts are much beyond ours, but He gives us discernment that we may understand. This is another reason we must be born-again, so we can see the kingdom of God. We must be born of water and Spirit in order to enter into it. The Spirit of God renews our mind. Our nature and thoughts do not appeal to the world. The closer we get to Jesus the more we become like Him. Prayer and fasting are ways to achieve our goals of hearing the still small voice of the Lord. If you don't believe the logos, or written word of God, you will not be able to receive a rhema, or personal living word from the Lord. When He speaks to you, it will line up with what the Bible says. We must know the Word of God, or Bible, so that we will not be deceived by Satan. *"Man shall not live by bread alone but by every word that proceedeth out of the mouth of God"* (Matthew 4:4). If we hunger for righteousness and thirst for knowledge and understanding, we shall be filled. Jesus came to give us power over the enemy. He also made it possible for us to go to heaven, a place of utopia, or paradise.

Receiving Revelation Knowledge

The Word of God was inspired by the Holy Spirit in the beginning. It will take the Holy Spirit to reveal the Word of God here in the last days. *"For the prophecy came not in old time by the will of man: but holy men of God spake as they were moved by the Holy Ghost"* (II Peter 1:21). *"All scripture is given by inspiration of God, and is profitable for doctrine, for reproof, for correction, for instruction in righteousness"* (II Timothy 3:16). *"The Word of God was conceived in the womb of a virgin by the Holy Ghost"* (Matthew 1:20). Jesus Christ is the Word of God. The Word came down from heaven and took on flesh. *"As many as receive Him, to them have been given the power to become the sons of God"* (John 1:12,14). *"For as many are led by the Spirit of God, they are the sons of God"* (Romans 8:14). We have been born again by the Spirit of God and revelation is given unto us, to guide us into all truth. The Spirit of God will even reveal to us things to come (John 16:13). The Spirit of God will always agree with the written Word of God, for He (the Spirit of God) has always revealed the Word of God. The Spirit revealed the Word (Jesus Christ), to John the Baptist.

John saw the Spirit come down in the form of a dove and land upon Jesus. John declared Jesus as the Lamb of God which has come to take away the sin of the world. Jesus had the Spirit of God from that day forward without measure (John 1:32, 35; 3:34). The apostle Peter received revelation from the Holy Spirit when he declared Jesus as "The Christ, the son of the Living God." Jesus then told Peter that flesh and blood had not revealed this unto him, but the Father which was in heaven. Jesus revealed to Peter, and unto us (the church) that this was the type of boldness and revelation He would build His church upon (Matthew 16: 16-18).

The apostle Paul stated, that we could receive the same kind of understanding of the mysteries of God as he had received, when we read the Word of God, because revelation comes by the Holy Spirit (Ephesians 3: 3-5). *"How that by revelation he made known unto me the mystery; (as I wrote afore in few words, whereby, when ye read, ye may understand my knowledge in the mystery of Christ) Which in other ages was not made known unto the sons of men, as it is now revealed unto his holy apostles and prophets by the Spirit"*. The Word of God is a mystery which is hid from the wise and prudent. We must be born-again to see the kingdom of God. This means that our eyes are opened once we receive Christ. We can read and hear the Word of God with understanding. We must be born of water and the Spirit to enter into the kingdom of God. *"Jesus answered and said unto him, Verily, verily, I say unto thee, Except a man be born again, he cannot see the kingdom of God. Nicodemus saith unto him, How can a man be born when he is old? Can he enter the second time into his mother's womb, and be born? Jesus answered,*

Verily, verily, I say unto thee, Except a man be born of water and of the Spirit, he cannot enter into the kingdom of God" (John 3: 3-5). Jesus was trying to teach us about a spiritual birth, not a natural birth. Jesus meant we must have our inner person renewed through faith. We understand that one day Jesus will return for us and we will enter His millennial kingdom. However, the kingdom of God is also in us. We should be entering into His presence every day. We must take advantage of every opportunity we have to read the Bible, or listen to it on tape, and assemble ourselves together at church. This kind of effort allows our mind, Spirit and heart to get saturated with the Word. Not only should we have a home church and attend revivals, we should also keep a revival spirit in our hearts. The Word of God is a sure word of prophecy. It must be our foundation. We must meditate on the scriptures and pray for understanding. If we do not know the Word of God, then we may have difficulty in recognizing what kind of spirit is speaking to us. *"Beloved, believe not every spirit, but try the spirits whether they are of God*" (I John 4:1). When we hear a voice speaking to us, either verbally, or inwardly, we must determine by the Word of God, if this is Jesus, Satan, or our own thoughts. Jesus said, *"My sheep know my voice, they will not follow another*" (John 10:3-5). The Holy Spirit will testify of Jesus and manifest Him to us. Once we've been born-again, we have the opportunity to receive more from the Lord. We can have as much of God as we desire. He will give us the desires of our heart. Let's desire more of Him.

Chapter Two

Seven Purposes of The Holy Spirit

The First Purpose Of The Holy Spirit

"But ye shall receive power, after that the Holy Ghost is come upon you: and ye shall be witnesses unto me both in Jerusalem, and in all Judaea, and in Samaria, and unto the uttermost part of the earth" (Acts 1:8). The first purpose of the Holy Spirit is to give us **power to be a witness.** We need boldness and authority to be an effective witness for Jesus. We have been given the great commission to go into all the world and preach the gospel. The Lord will use us to be a voice crying in the wilderness. He will empower us to do the job. This is called the anointing. We need the anointing to break yokes, not only in other people's lives, but also in ours. *"And it shall come to pass in that day, that his burden shall be taken away from off thy shoulder, and his yoke from off thy neck, and the yoke shall be destroyed because of the anointing"* (Isaiah 10:27). Yokes of bondage and burdens hinder our ability to be a better witness. Many people are shy

and timid. Some are afraid to look other people in the eyes. The Holy Spirit comes into our life when we are born-again and helps us to be bold. The anointing breaks the spirit of fear. *"For God hath not given us the spirit of fear; but of power, and of love, and of a sound mind"* (II Timothy 1:7). God has not only saved us, but He has also called us for a divine purpose. He has called, chosen, and justified us. God's Spirit helps us to fulfill His mission. Jesus was anointed to destroy the works of the enemy. The Holy Spirit gives us courage to speak up and testify. We are overcomers by the blood of the Lamb and by the word of our testimony. *"And they overcame him by the blood of the Lamb, and by the word of their testimony"* (Revelation 12:11). We need the power of God to destroy the works of the enemy. It takes the anointing to live holy and overcome evil. The steps to receiving power in our life is repentance, then baptism of water and of the Spirit. We must exercise our faith by using it. Faith without works is dead. A believer's faith increases as they hear the Word of God preached, or, as they read the Word of God. *"So then faith cometh by hearing, and hearing by the word of God"* (Romans 10:17). Signs follow the believer. *"And these signs shall follow them that believe; In my name shall they cast out devils; they shall speak with new tongues; They shall take up serpents; and if they drink any deadly thing, it shall not hurt them; they shall lay hands on the sick, and they shall recover"* (Mark 16:17, 18). God always confirms His word with signs following. If we speak the Word of God, the Lord will bring it to pass. Jesus gives us the power, or ability, to be an effective witness. We should be a witness everywhere we go. I had family members who were believers that prayed for me. In 1986, I was involved in a head-on collision automobile wreck. I was in a coma for 27 days. My family laid hands on me and prayed the prayer of faith. *" Is any sick among you? let him call for the elders of the church; and let them pray over him, anointing him with oil in the name of the Lord. And the prayer of faith shall save the sick, and the Lord shall raise him up; and if he have committed sins, they shall be forgiven him"* (James 5:14). Jesus came to me and raised me up from my death bed. (Be sure and get the 100 page book of my testimony mentioned on the last page). The anointing empowers us to speak the Word as a witness. The anointing also performs healings and miracles through us that believe. The Word of God always works. It will never fail. The Holy Spirit brings the word to pass. The anointing makes every believer powerful. God wants to use His body of believers to show forth signs and wonders. God reveals to the world that He is real, through us the believers. The world sees the power of God through our lives. When we exercise our faith to believe God for the impossible, it pleases God. The Lord moves by His Spirit to answer our request. The Holy Spirit is God's will in action. If we ask anything according to His will, He is obligated to answer. We only have to have patience and wait on the Lord. The Holy Spirit will move for us. God does things by His Spirit. *" Then he answered and spake unto me, saying, This is the word of the LORD unto Zerubbabel, saying, Not by might, nor by power, but by my spirit, saith the LORD of hosts"* (Zechariah 4:6). We should always give God the praise and glory for everything the Holy Spirit does. Everything that the Lord does is good. If we love the Lord, we will keep His commandments. We should never grieve the Holy Ghost, but allow Him to work through us. We recognize the Holy Spirit as one of the three manifestations of the God head. *"For there are three that bear record in heaven, the Father, the Word, and the Holy Ghost: and these three are one*" (I John 5:7). Jesus is the Word of God who was conceived in a virgin by the Holy Spirit. "*Now the birth of Jesus Christ was on this wise: When as his mother Mary was espoused to Joseph, before they came together, she was found with child of the Holy Ghost*" (Matthew 1:18). "*Behold, a virgin shall be with child, and shall bring forth a son, and they shall call his name Emmanuel, which being interpreted is, God with us*" (Matthew 1:23). Mary was pregnant with the Word of God. We should allow the Holy Spirit to empower us with the Word of God. The Lord wants to birth a new life in you by His Spirit. "*But as many as received him, to them gave he power to become the sons of God, even to them that believe on his name: which were born, not of blood, nor of the will of the flesh, nor of the will of man, but of God*" (John 1:12,13). We are begotten of the Word of God and born of His Spirit. When Jesus walked this earth full of the Holy Ghost between the years 27 A.D. and 30 A.D., He always directed the glory to His Father. After Jesus ascended back to the third heaven, the Holy Ghost came down to lift up Jesus. If we lift up Jesus, He will draw all men unto Him by His Spirit. We must be drawn by the Holy Spirit to be saved. If someone hears about Jesus, He will draw them to repentance. He will compel them to learn of Him. The power is in the name of Jesus. Every believer will always speak the name of Jesus. The believer has been given power of attorney from God to use His name. When we speak the name of Jesus, diseases and sicknesses of all manner must step back. I hope you are full of the Spirit and power of God, and you are doing great exploits through His name.

"And he saith unto them, Ye shall drink indeed of my cup, and be baptized with the baptism that I am baptized with" (Matthew 20:23a). Jesus began healing the sick and performing other great miracles after He received the fullness for the Holy Spirit. We also need the baptism of the Holy Spirit for God to work miracles through us.

The Second Purpose Of The Holy Spirit

The Holy Spirit will **manifest** or reveal Jesus to us. *"He that hath my commandments, and keepeth them, he it is that loveth me: and he that loveth me shall be loved of my Father, and I will love him, and will manifest myself to him"* (John 14:21). People are watching us to see if we have the goods -so to speak. The Holy Spirit will manifest Jesus to us and through us. Our best testimony is how we live our lives for Jesus. When we are born-again, we take on God's nature. The Holy Spirit reveals the fruit of the Spirit to us and through us if we allow Him to. *"But the fruit of the Spirit is love, joy, peace, longsuffering, gentleness, goodness, faith, meekness, temperance: against such there is no law. And they that are Christ's have crucified the flesh with the affections and lusts"* (Galatians 5:22-24). These attributes should manifest in our life. The Holy Spirit will help us walk in the fruit of the Spirit. The works of the flesh are not of God. *"Now the works of the flesh are manifest, which are these; Adultery, fornication, uncleanness, lasciviousness, Idolatry, witchcraft, hatred, variance, emulations, wrath, strife, seditions, heresies, Envyings, murders, drunkenness, revellings, and such like: of the which I tell you before, as I have also told you in time past, that they which*

39

do such things shall not inherit the kingdom of God"
(Galatians 5:19-21). We must listen to the Holy Spirit and stay in
the Word of God to live in the Spirit. We will win people to Jesus
with love. The love of God will never fail. Jesus is love. Perfect
love casts out all fear. The Holy Spirit will manifest the
characteristics of Jesus in us.

The Third Purpose Of The Holy Spirit

The Holy Spirit wants to teach us all things. "*But the Comforter,
which is the Holy Ghost, whom the Father will send in my
name, he shall teach you all things, and bring all things to
your remembrance, whatsoever I have said unto you*" (John
14:26). The Holy Spirit will bring all that we learn back to our
remembrance. The Holy Spirit knows all things. If we listen to
Him, we will know what to do in every situation. "*But ye have
an unction from the Holy One, and ye know all things.
But the anointing which ye have received of him abideth
in you, and ye need not that any man teach you: but as the
same anointing teacheth you of all things, and is truth,
and is no lie, and even as it hath taught you, ye shall abide
in him*" (I John 2:20, 27). The Apostle John is not saying that
we should not sit under good teachers. John is just saying that the
Holy Spirit can teach us much more in a shorter length of time.
The Holy Spirit can say or teach more in five minutes than a man
or woman can say or teach in five days. America is so blessed
with Bible colleges. Many Bible colleges however, will never
teach about the fullness of the Holy Spirit. You have already read
more information about the Spirit of the Living God than some
Professors have ever read. Some may have read about this
information, but we must act upon it. We must believe that the

fullness of the Holy Spirit is for us today. The Apostle Paul prayed for the church at Ephesus to be strengthened by the Holy Spirit. He stated that there were depths in God and in the knowledge of God. He wanted all saints to be filled with all the fullness of God. *"That he would grant you, according to the riches of his glory, to be strengthened with might by his Spirit in the inner man; That Christ may dwell in your hearts by faith; that ye, being rooted and grounded in love May be able to comprehend with all saints what is the breadth, and length, and depth, and height; And to know the love of Christ, which passeth knowledge, that ye might be filled with all the fullness of God "* (Ephesians 3:16-19). In order for the Holy Spirit to teach us, we must be willing to learn. He wants us to receive the spirit of wisdom, and revelation in the knowledge of Him. The eyes of our understanding should be enlightened by the Holy Spirit. (Ephesians 1:17, 18). The Holy Spirit will renew our minds so we can learn of the Lord. We don't have to worry about trying to quote the whole Bible from Genesis to the maps. We just need to study to show ourselves approved of God. If we apply ourselves to the Word of God, either through reading or listening, it will be planted as a seed in our heart. The Holy Spirit will then bring back to our remembrance what we need to know. As we meditate on the Word of God, we will receive revelation knowledge. The Holy Spirit will reveal danger to us, or, other soon to happen events. He should be a part of our everyday life at home, work, and during leisure activities. He knows what's in our future. He will keep us safe and help us prosper. It is God's will for us to be in health and prosper and learn of Him. *"Beloved, I wish above all things that thou mayest prosper and be in health, even as thy soul prospereth"* (III John V.2). There are

41

some people who think God wants them to be sick, broke and dumb. But this is contrary to the word of God. They will never know any different unless they become meek and teachable. God does not put sickness on us to teach us something. He does chasten us if we don't obey Him. This reveals that He loves us. *"Now no chastening for the present seemeth to be joyous, but grievous: nevertheless afterward it yieldeth the peaceable fruit of righteousness unto them which are exercised thereby"* (Hebrews 12:11). He can remove His peace from us and immediately He has our attention. God may allow us to get sick, but he does not put it on us. We are His children. He loves us with an everlasting love. His Spirit comforts us. We don't put diseases on our children to teach them a lesson and neither does our heavenly Father. Some people have been taught wrong about healings and miracles. I started to pray for a lady in a wheelchair one time. I told her that Jesus had raised me up out of a wheelchair, and that He was no respector of persons. She said there was no need to pray for her to be healed of the bone disease, because God had put it on her to teach her something. I ask her how long had she been in the wheelchair with the disease. She said about seven years. I then told her in a nice way that she must be a slow learner. She said that nothing would help her get better. So I ask her if she was taking medication for her illness, and she said yes. I then asked her why did she take medication to remove the sickness, if God had put it on her, as she assumed. After she begin to realize that she had falsely accused God, she then allowed me to pray with her. I am not against doctors, but sometimes they do not have the answers. We have a great physician in Jesus. I told the lady of others who had walked out of wheelchairs and who had been healed of diseases through faith in the name of Jesus. But she did not arise and walk. I have never seen her since, but God used me to teach her the truth. If we would only get a hold of the Word of God. Peter said that Jesus had taken a beating for our healing. *"Who his own self bare our sins in his own body on the tree, that we, being dead to sins, should live unto righteousness: by whose stripes ye were healed"* (I Peter 2:24). Some people do not want the Holy Spirit to teach them anything because, *"To whom much is given, much is required"* (Luke 12:48b). Jesus received thirty nine stripes across His back for our healing. Scientist now say there are thirty nine categories of diseases. Jesus new this all along. The Holy Spirit will always speak the truth, and what He says will agree with the Word of God. A man once said the Holy Spirit told him the very day that Jesus would return. This however goes directly against the Word of God. *"But of that day and hour knoweth no man, no, not the angels of heaven, but my Father only"* (Matthew 24:36). We must learn the written Word of God in order to trust the voice we are listening to. Remember, the true Holy Spirit will never teach or say anything contrary to the Word of God.

The Fourth Purpose Of The Holy Spirit

"Peace I leave with you, my peace I give unto you: not as the world giveth, give I unto you. Let not your heart be troubled, neither let it be afraid" (John 14:27). God wants you and I to have peace in our mind and spirit. Satan wants us to be fearful and full of doubt. We can have the peace of God. This kind of peace goes beyond man's understanding. The world has no peace and therefore it can not offer any peace. *"For when they shall say, Peace and safety; then sudden destruction*

cometh upon them, as travail upon a woman with child; and they shall not escape" (I Thessalonians 5:3). It does not matter how many peace treaties are signed by the world governments, they will all fail to achieve total peace. The United Nations was formed in 1947 to establish peace on Earth. It has helped in some areas, but the ultimate peace is in Christ Jesus. Jesus said in John 14:1 "*Let not your hearts be troubled*". He stated that in the world we would have tribulations, but to be of good cheer, he had overcome the world. "*These things I have spoken unto you, that in me ye might have peace*" (John 16:33). It feels good to be able to lie in bed at night and not have to worry about everything that is going on in the world. We must leave it up to the Lord to straighten everything out, because we sure can't. If we watch the evening news all the time, we will become discouraged. All they tell about is bad things that are happening. That does not edify us. Not that we should tune out everything that is going on.

We understand things are going to happen, but God is in control. His Spirit is here to comfort and encourage us. We should choose to see the positive things that are going on around us, rather than all the negative. The Lord will see that we are clothed and fed. If we are not happy and content with what we have, then we will become sad and covetous. I have ministered in countries outside the U.S. nineteen times between 1993 and 1997. I have seen alot of poor, hungry people. The Holy Spirit wants to whisper to them and say, those who suffer with Christ will reign with Christ. We have it so good here in the U.S.A. Let's pray for peace to come to our brothers and sisters in Christ who are not so fortunate. Many are the afflictions of the righteous, but God delivers us out of them all. The thief comes to kill, steal, and destroy. Jesus has come to give life, and restoration. Once we understand that death cannot hold us, and Satan cannot defeat us, we have the battle nearly won. If God be for us, who can be against us. We are overcomers through the Holy Ghost. We can do all things through Christ Jesus who strengthens us. *"Depart from evil, and do good; seek peace, and pursue it"* (Psalm 34:14). If we seek for peace, then it can be found. If we ask for peace we shall obtain it. We are told to pray for the peace of Jerusalem in Psalm 122:6 *"Pray for the peace of Jerusalem: they shall prosper that love thee"*. Only in the millennial reign shall Israel obtain total peace. The peace accords that are being signed between Israel and other middle East countries will not last. Only when Jesus, the Prince of Peace, returns at the end of The Great Tribulation with His saints, shall Israel and the rest of the world see real peace. (Be sure to get a copy of my book on End-Time events offered on the last page). Proverbs 3:2 says that through the Word of God and keeping God's commandments we shall add length of days, long life and peace for ourselves. Blessed are the peace-makers, for they shall obtain peace. We must allow the Holy Spirit to help us be kind one to another. He will help us turn the other cheek if someone offends us. Without peace and holiness no man shall see the Lord. *"Follow peace with all men, and holiness, without which no man shall see the Lord"* (Hebrews 12:14). If we forgive others, the Spirit of peace and love shall overshadow us. To be spiritually minded is life and peace. *"Be careful for nothing; but in every thing by prayer and supplication with thanksgiving let your requests be made known unto God. And the peace of God, which passeth all understanding, shall keep your hearts and minds through Christ Jesus"* (Philippians 4:6,7).

The Fifth Purpose Of The Holy Spirit

The fifth purpose of the Holy Spirit is to **bear witness** with our spirit that we are a child of God. The Holy Spirit will quicken our mortal body. *"But if the Spirit of him that raised up Jesus from the dead dwell in you, he that raised up Christ from the dead shall also <u>quicken your mortal bodies by his Spirit</u> that dwelleth in you. For ye have not received the spirit of bondage again to fear; but ye have received the Spirit of adoption, whereby we cry, Abba, Father. <u>The Spirit itself beareth witness with our spirit</u>, that we are the children of God"* (Romans 8:11, 15, 16).

God wants us to know, that we know, that we know, that He is in us. The Holy Spirit delivers us from condemnation and the law of sin and death. The closer we get to Jesus, the more we feel His presence. There is nothing in the world like feeling the presence of God. It may feel like liquid love or an unexplainable warm sensation flowing through your body. When we realize we have a Heavenly Father who loves and cares for us, the Holy Spirit leaps inside of us. He bears witness with our spirit that this is true. Yes God is real, and this is how I know; as I worship the Lord, I can feel Him in my soul. We as Christians have been adopted into the family of God. We are joint-heirs with our elder brother, Christ Jesus. We have privileges as the heirs of salvation. We are just waiting for that final day in which we will receive a new glorified body. The Holy Spirit helps us to be obedient children. We walk after the Spirit, and not after the flesh. The Spirit of God inside us will guide and direct our path. He will bear witness that we are doing what He has called us to do. The flesh is an enemy to the will of God. The flesh wants to be continually satisfied. But, we mortify the deeds of the flesh and follow the Holy Spirit. Sometimes the anointing of God is so strong on our mortal bodies it makes our skin crawl, or get goose bumps. I started calling them Holy Ghost bumps because a goose has got nothing to do with it. I was once in a world of sin. I was on drugs and alcohol. I wanted to feel something, and I wanted to be wanted. I needed attention. Now I can come into the presence of Jesus, by His Spirit. He gives me all the love and attention that I desire. Now I am addicted to Jesus. I used to get on drugs to get on cloud nine - so to speak. Now I am filled with the Holy Spirit. I can get drunk in the Spirit, and I feel like I'm walking on nine clouds! We can worship the Lord without fear, worry, and condemnation. *"For as many as are led by the Spirit of God, they are the sons of God"* (Romans 8:14). We will never take the place of Jesus who is the Son of God. However, we do have a rightful place of kinship in God. If we listen to the Holy Spirit and allow Him to lead us, we become sons of God. In other words, obedient children. Are you a child of God? We should be led by the Holy Spirit to help our family grow everyday. Let the Holy Spirit shake you. He will stir up the gifts within us. There is a great shaking and stirring taking place right now. Stir up yourself and war with the prophecies that have been given you. Every word shall be established by the mouth of two or three witnesses.

The Sixth Purpose Of The Holy Spirit

The sixth purpose of the Holy Spirit is to **help us to pray in the Spirit**. God wants us to pray for his divine will to be done. I have covered in pages past about the baptism of the Holy Ghost. Jude said we could build ourselves up praying in the Holy Ghost. *"But ye, beloved, building up yourselves on your most holy faith,* *praying in the Holy Ghost*" (Jude V.20). "*And not only they, but ourselves also, which have the firstfruits of the Spirit, even we ourselves groan within ourselves, waiting for the adoption, to wit, the redemption of our body. Likewise the Spirit also helpeth our infirmities: for we know not what we should pray for as we ought: but the Spirit itself maketh intercession for us with groanings which cannot be uttered. And he that searcheth the hearts knoweth what is the mind of the Spirit, because he maketh intercession for the saints according to the will of God*" (Romans 8:23, 26, 27). God wants us to become Holy Ghost prayer warriors. We need to be intercessors who will allow the Holy Spirit to speak out of us. When we pray in the Spirit, we are edifying ourselves. We are also allowing the Lord to ask Himself to do something for us or someone else. After Jesus was filled with the Holy Ghost, He became an intercessor. Jesus raised a little girl from the dead through intercessory prayer. It was Jairus, a ruler of the synagogue, whose daughter died. Jesus went to her and prayed in the Spirit and she arose. "*And he took the damsel by the hand, and said unto her, Talitha cumi; which is, being interpreted, Damsel, I say unto thee, arise. And straightway the damsel arose, and walked*" (Mark 5:41,42a). Some have said the words Talitha Cumi is Aramaic, while others have said it is Latin. Either way, Jesus was Hebrew, therefore He spoke the Hebrew language. The Word of God clearly says in verse 41 "which is being interpreted, Damsel, I say unto thee, arise". This is tongues and interpretation. Jesus was speaking in the Spirit to this young girl who was dead. He spoke in resurrection power. Some want to argue the point, but it is clearly in the Bible. Another instance where Jesus prayed in the Spirit, is when He raised Lazarus from the dead. *"When Jesus therefore saw her weeping, and the Jews also weeping which came with her, he groaned in the spirit, and was troubled. Jesus therefore again groaning in himself cometh to the grave. It was a cave, and a stone lay upon it. Then they took away the stone from the place where the dead was laid. And Jesus lifted up his eyes, and said, Father, I thank thee that thou hast heard me"* (John 11:33,38,41). Jesus not only groaned in the Spirit, but He thanked the Father for hearing Him pray. Romans 8:26 says the Holy Spirit makes intercession through us with groanings that can not be understood. The apostle Paul said in I Corinthians 14:2 *"For he that speaketh in an unknown tongue speaketh not unto men, but unto God: for no man understandeth him; howbeit in the Spirit he speaketh mysteries"*. The third time scripture reveals Jesus speaking in other tongues is when He was dying on the cross. *"And about the ninth hour Jesus cried with a loud voice, saying, Eli, Eli, lama sabachthani? that is to say, My God, my God, why hast thou forsaken me"* (Matthew 27:46). This was a prophecy being fulfilled from Psalms 22:1. Many standing by thought He was calling on Elias. This reveals they did not understand the language. Jesus was calling on the Father. Jesus at that moment was taking on the world of sin so you and I could be free. Jesus only spoke a few words in another language, but it was effective. A creative language came forth from Jesus. When the Holy Spirit descended upon the Word of God (Jesus), a force came forth that mankind had never seen before. All things had been created by Jesus, and for Jesus, even in the beginning. *"The same was in the beginning with God. All things were made by him; and without him was not anything made that was made"* (John 1:2-3). Some people are not aware that Jesus existed before he was born in a manger. However, Jesus was there when creation began. He is the Alpha and Omega, the beginning and the end. " *In the beginning was the Word, and the Word was with God, and the Word was God*" (John 1:1). "*Saying, I am Alpha and Omega, the first and the last*" (Revelation 1:11a). When Jesus spoke to the boisterous winds and the raging sea, they became calm. "*But as they sailed he fell asleep: and there came down a storm of wind on the lake; and they were filled with water, and were in jeopardy. And they came to him, and awoke him, saying, Master, master, we perish. Then he arose, and rebuked the wind and the raging of the water: and they ceased, and there was a calm. And he said unto them, Where is your faith? And they being afraid wondered, saying one to another, What manner of man is this! for he commandeth even the winds and water, and they obey him*" (Luke 8:23-25). The wind and the sea recognized that creative voice. Mother nature had to bow to the Creator. After the great flood of Noah's day, men began building a tower to reach to heaven. Everyone had the same identical language. They had come together for a purpose. Man is always trying to get to heaven his own way. But we must go through Jesus. He is the only way. He is the door. Anyone who tries to get to heaven another way is a thief and a robber. "*Verily, verily, I say unto you, He that entereth not by the door into the sheepfold, but climbeth up some other way, the same is a thief and a robber*" (John 10:1). If the people of God ever realize who they are in Christ Jesus, and come together in one mind and one accord, nothing shall be withheld from them. "*And the whole earth was of one language, and of one speech. And they said, Go to, let us build us a city and a tower, whose top may reach unto heaven; And the LORD said, Behold, the people is one, and they have all one language; and this they begin to do: and now nothing will be restrained from them, which they have imagined to do"* (Genesis 11:1,4a,6). There is power in unity. It is good when the brethren can dwell together in unity. I see the church of the Living God coming together more now than ever before. The Apostle Paul said in Ephesians chapter four that the five fold ministry had be given to edify and perfect the church until we come into the unity of the faith. *"And he gave some, apostles; and some, prophets; and some, evangelists; and some, pastors and teachers; For the perfecting of the saints, for the work of the ministry, for the edifying of the body of Christ: Till we all come in the unity of the faith, and of the knowledge of the Son of God, unto a perfect man, unto the measure of the stature of the fulness of Christ"* (Ephesians 4:11-13). Revival has begun to break out all over the world. The army of God is being raised up and filled with the anointing. Some people are confused about the outpouring of the Holy Ghost. People were confused on the day of Pentecost, but it did not stop God from pouring His Spirit out. *"Now when this was noised abroad, the multitude came together, and were confounded, because that every man heard them speak in his own language"* (Acts 2:6). I have never met anyone who has experienced Pentecost in their life and doubted it. I never believed in miracles and healings until it happened in my life. I was not sure if the baptism of the Holy Spirit was for me in the beginning. So I asked the Lord to fill me if this gift was still real, and if it was for me. And He did. Praise God! In Genesis chapter eleven, God came down to confound man's language and scatter him abroad. *"Go to, let us go down, and there confound their language, that they may not understand one another's speech. So the LORD scattered them abroad from thence upon the face of all the earth: and they left off to build the city. Therefore is the name of it called Babel; because the LORD did there confound the language of all the earth: and from thence did the LORD scatter them abroad upon the face of all the earth"* (Genesis 11:7-9). When the day of Pentecost arrived in Acts chapter two, the Holy Spirit was giving man the opportunity to speak in one language once again. This is the unknown tongue, or, God's language. Angel's have a language, man has languages, and the Lord has a language. When we pray in the Spirit, we are not scattering, or being scattered, but we are building up and edifying the body of Christ. We are the temple of the Holy Ghost. We the believers are building a temple to heaven, and God is with us. We are going through Jesus. We are his temple. We are the body and Jesus is the head. Except the Lord build a house, they that labor, labor in vain. We want Jesus to approve of everything we do for Him. Multitudes of Christians will go to heaven empty handed. They do not want power, nor the anointing. There are thousands of Christians who love Jesus and keep His commandments. They are faithful to go to church and they are good moral people. However, they are not anointed, nor do they have any power. This is there choice, not the Lord's. We need to examine ourselves to see if we are satisfied where we are at with God. God is not a man that He should lie. If He said this power is available to us, then we should receive it. If we seek God now, we will find Him. *"Ho, every one that thirsteth, come ye to the waters, and he that hath no money; come ye, buy, and eat; yea, come, buy wine and milk without money and without price. Seek ye the LORD while he may be found, call ye upon him while he is near"* (Isaiah 55:1,6). Don't be confused about the Holy Spirit. God is not the author of confusion - man is. Man continually confuses himself, because he tries to analyze in the natural, the spiritual things of God. Many men have dissected the Word of God and removed what they do not like or understand. But if it is in the Word of God, we had better receive it and walk in the truth thereof, if we want life. Jesus said, *"I have come that they might have life and that they may have it more abundantly"* (John 10:10b). Some Christians are just enduring their salvation, while others are really enjoying theirs. The Lord said in Zechariah chapter ten that we should ask of Him to pour His Spirit out on us in the latter days. *"Ask ye of the LORD rain in the time of the latter rain; so the LORD shall make bright clouds, and give them showers of rain, to every one grass in the field"* (Zechariah 10:1). He is not just speaking of natural rain , but also of a spiritual rain. We need to get under the glory spout, where the anointing is being poured out. We have to ask to receive. Believe and you shall receive. Pray in the Spirit and with understanding. Let those tongues of fire flow in the river. Gideon and three-hundred men were used to defeat the enemies of Israel in Judges chapter seven. Gideon was chosen by God, even though he did not feel worthy. We are worthy because of the blood of Jesus. Whom the Lord chooses, he justifies. We are mighty sons and daughters of valor. Don't look at your past. If you've been born-again, it's covered in the precious blood of Jesus. Don't look at your disadvantages, look at how big your God is. Before Gideon and three-hundred men were used, there had to come a separation of who wanted to fight and who did not. Thirty-one thousand seven-hundred men went home.

Gideon and three-hundred others were getting their tongues in the water. *"So he brought down the people unto the water: and the LORD said unto Gideon, Every one that lappeth of the water with his tongue, as a dog lappeth, him shalt thou set by himself; likewise every one that boweth down upon his knees to drink. And the number of them that lapped, putting their hand to their mouth, were three hundred men: but all the rest of the people bowed down upon their knees to drink water. And the LORD said unto Gideon, By the three hundred men that lapped will I save you, and deliver the Midianites into thine hand"* (Judges 7:5-7). The water represents the Holy Spirit. If you will get your tongue in the water, or in the Spirit, you will have tongues of fire. *"And there appeared unto them cloven tongues like as of fire, and it sat upon each of them"* (Acts 2:3). James chapter three reveals that the tongue can no man tame. *"And the tongue is a fire, a world of iniquity: so is the tongue among our members, that it defileth the whole body But the tongue can no man tame; it is an unruly evil, full of deadly poison. Therewith bless we God, even the Father; and therewith curse we men, which are made after the similitude of God. Out of the same mouth proceedeth blessing and cursing. My brethren, these things ought not so to be"* (James 3:6, 8-10). The only way we can tame our tongue is to be full of the Holy Spirit. He is the bridle that we need to keep us in check. Life and death is in the tongue. Let your tongue bring forth much fruit. Be kind to one another, and bless each other. *"A man's belly shall be satisfied with the fruit of his mouth; and with the increase of his lips shall he be filled. Death and life are in the power of the tongue: and they that love it shall eat the fruit thereof*" (Proverbs 18:20-21). The power of God is within us, but we need love to help us win the lost. If we have faith to move mountains, and are willing to give our body as a sacrifice, it is nothing if we don't have love. Faith, hope, and love, go hand in hand with the anointing. The greatest of these is love. *"Though I speak with the tongues of men and of angels, and have not charity, I am become as sounding brass, or a tinkling cymbal. And though I have the gift of prophecy, and understand all mysteries, and all knowledge; and though I have all faith, so that I could remove mountains, and have not charity, I am nothing. And though I bestow all my goods to feed the poor, and though I give my body to be burned, and have not charity, it profiteth me nothing*" (I Corinthians 13:1-3). The word charity is the same word as love. When a Christian receives the baptism of the Holy Spirit, they may only say a few words. However, some may speak in other tongues for quite some time. The Lord will help us to become mature in the Spirit. *"Whom shall he teach knowledge? and whom shall he make to understand doctrine? them that are weaned from the milk, and drawn from the breasts. For precept must be upon precept, precept upon precept; line upon line, line upon line; here a little, and there a little: For with stammering lips and another tongue will he speak to this people*" (Isaiah 28:9-11). We must rightly divide the Word of God. All of us share what little knowledge we have received from the Lord. We pool our revelation of knowledge together and we grow thereby. When I first received the baptism of the Holy Spirit, Satan told me it was not real. Then I realized he had told me the same thing about salvation. Satan is a liar.

Whatever he says, it is just the opposite. He told me I was saying something bad in another language. But the Holy Spirit told me to read I Corinthians 12:3 which says: *"**Wherefore I give you to understand, that no man speaking by the Spirit of God calleth Jesus accursed: and that no man can say that Jesus is the Lord, but by the Holy Ghost**"*. I then realized I could not say anything bad in the Holy Spirit. Satan then told me my prayer language did not sound like most others. The Holy Spirit then said He gave us our very own prayer language. It did not have to sound like someone else's. A man told me one day after I had witnessed to him that I could not have the Holy Spirit baptism like the disciples did in the Bible. I told him he was to late, I had already received this precious gift. The man then said it was of the devil (which is a common remark among non-Pentecostal people). I told the man three reasons why this gift could not be of the devil. 1. It was in the Bible; 2. It was something good. All good things come from above; 3. I had served the devil for twenty-four years in night clubs and pool halls and I had never spoken in tongues. He did not know quite what to say. If this experience had been of the devil, he and I both realized that I would have had this experience a long time ago. If Satan cast out Satan how can he stand. This gift of the Holy Ghost is of God. You must experience it for yourself. It is your tongue and your voice that the Holy Spirit will use. You just have to learn how to yield to the Spirit. The Lord has people praying for you right now that you have never met before. They are praying for the divine will of God to occur in your life. They are praying in the Spirit. If you have prayed in the Spirit before, there is no telling who you may have prayed for. I went to speak at a drug rehab clinic once in 1986. When I arrived, a young man came up to me and asked me if I was their speaker, and I said yes. He asked me if I believed in praying in the Spirit, and I said yes. He then said that the Holy Spirit had awaken him on April 13th, 1986 at 6:45 a.m. on a Sunday morning. He was compelled to pray in the Spirit all that day. The Lord told him that one day he would meet who he had been praying and interceeding for. I then looked at him and shook his hand and thanked him for praying for me. I then told him that I was pronounced dead-on-arrival at Vanderbilt University hospital on April 13th 1986. God used him to interceed for me until my family could get there and anoint me with oil. The leading trauma physician later told me that he was sending me to the morgue but something told him to do whatever he could. I had a torn aorta artery, a ruptured spleen, broken ankle, hip and jaw. I was given 124 units of blood, my kidney's and liver stopped functioning. They waited 25 days to repair my broken bones. While I laid in a coma, Jesus came to me and touched my head. He spoke to me and told me to go and tell His people that He was coming soon and that He was still the miracle worker. I had several believers in my family that anointed me with oil and prayed the prayer of faith. Thank God for intercessory prayer.

The Seventh Purpose Of The Holy Spirit

The seventh purpose of the Holy Spirit is to **operate the gifts through us**. When we pray in the Spirit it goes directly to God. There is no need for an interpretation from someone else if we are praying to the Lord. An interpretation of tongues is when a message is coming from God to the body of Christ. If a message is given out in tongues, to the church, then there should be an interpretation.

Now a person who gives out a message in tongues may be also used to interpret. *"I would that ye all spake with tongues, but rather that ye prophesied: for greater is he that prophesieth than he that speaketh with tongues, except he interpret, that the church may receive edifying"* (I Corinthians 14:5). However, in most instances the Holy Spirit will give out a message through a believer, and someone else will interpret. If there be no interpreter in the midst, then that person is to pray silently to themselves in the Spirit. *"If any man speak in an unknown tongue, let it be by two, or at the most by three, and that by course; and let one interpret. But if there be no interpreter, let him keep silence in the church; and let him speak to himself, and to God"* (I Corinthians 14:27-28). We can only learn as much as our teacher knows. It is very important to sit under good anointed teachers. When you want to learn, you go to where it is taught. If you want to know more about the Holy Spirit and how to flow in the gifts of the Spirit, then you must get in a good anointed Holy Ghost church. It is sad to say, but a majority of congregations hear the same message or the same theme every service. If everyone in the congregation is already saved, then why preach on salvation every service? If everyone is baptized in the Holy Spirit, then why preach on the baptism of the Holy Ghost? There are nine gifts of the Holy Spirit. All nine gifts are worked by the same Holy Spirit. There are different manifestations of the Holy Spirit, but, it is the same Spirit that works them all. *"Now there are diversities of gifts, but the same Spirit. And there are differences of administrations, but the same Lord. And there are diversities of operations, but it is the same God which worketh all in all. But the manifestation of the Spirit is given to every man to profit withal"* (I Corinthians 12:4-7). Here are the nine gifts of the Spirit listed in I Corinthians 12: 8-11. *"For to one is given by the Spirit the word of wisdom; to another the word of knowledge by the same Spirit; to another faith by the same Spirit; to another the gifts of healing by the same Spirit; to another the working of miracles; to another prophecy; to another discerning of spirits; to another divers kinds of tongues; to another the interpretation of tongues: But all these worketh that one and the selfsame Spirit, dividing to every man severally as he will. For as the body is one, and hath many members, and all the members of that one body, being many, are one body: so also is Christ"* The Apostle Paul mentioned that one day tongues would cease, knowledge shall be done away with, and even prophecies would fail. When we enter into the millennial reign of Christ, we will not need miracles healings, tongues, or even preaching. But at this time knowledge has not been done away with, and tongues have not ceased. Personal prophecies will fail because man is involved. If someone is given a word of prophecy, it can be conditional. They may have to do something besides just warring with the prophecy. For instance, if someone is told that God is about to bless them with a new job, they may need to put job applications in, etc.... Please read I Corinthians chapters 12 through 14. These chapters were written for instruction about the Holy Spirit. Some have suggested that perhaps the baptism of the Holy Spirit ceased with the last apostles. However, apostles are still here today. In fact Paul gives a list of eight positions that God has put in the church. *"And God hath set some in the church, first apostles, secondarily prophets, thirdly teachers, after that miracles, then gifts of healings, helps, governments, diversities of tongues"* (I Corinthians 12:28). Many churches recongnize teachers, helps, and governments but we need the operation of all of these positions to move on toward perfection.

I pray that this book will in some way help whosoever reads it. May the Lord bless you in all your endeavors to draw closer to him. *"Draw nigh to God, and he will draw nigh to you"* (James 5:8). *"He that believeth on me, as the scripture hath said, out of his belly shall flow rivers of living water; (But this spake he of the Spirit, which they that believe on him should receive: for the Holy Ghost was not yet given; because that Jesus was not yet glorified)"* (John 8:38-39). Jesus has now ascended up and been glorified. He has received the glory that He had in the beginning. You now can have the fullness of the Holy Spirit!

Prayer To Be Born Again

*Father, I come to You in the name of Your son, Jesus Christ, confessing with my mouth and believing in my heart according to Your Word in **Romans 10:9** that Jesus died for my sins and was dead three days. Father, You raised Jesus from the dead and now He intercedes in my behalf. I am a sinner and I have fallen short of the glory of God, but I am a sinner and I have fallen short fo the glory of God, but I am now being rasied up with Christ and I am born again. I repent of all my sins and I shall be baptized in the Name of the Lord and I shall receive the gift of the Holy Ghost according to Acts 2:38. I proclaim the precious blood of Jesus over my soul and I am saved. I will testify that Jesus is Lord of Lords and King of Kings forever in my life. Thank You Father for writing my name down in the Lamb's Book of Life. I am redeemed from the curse of the law and the sin of death. I now have enternal life because I believe.*

Amen.

60

Book Order List

*A Miracle In
The Making*

"A Miracle In The Making" The story of Evangelist Richard Madison's healing and conversion to the Lord, is living proof of God's promises, resurrection and power. From death to a full-time teaching and healing ministry, Richard is truly one of God's chosen people. Let Richard show you how you can have miracles in your life. In God's eyes, nothing in your life is impossible.

Sales Price - $7.00
Cassette Tape Only - $4.00
Video Tape Only - $15.00
All Three Items - $25.00

*Signs Of Jesus' Return
Are You Ready?*

"Howbeit when He, the Spirit of Truth, is come, He will come, He will guide you into all truth: for He shall not speak of Himself; but whatsoever He shall hear that shall He speak: and He will show you things to come" (John 16:13). God wants to reveal mysteries to His people. Although the Lord will never reveal the day nor the hour of His Return, we are able to discern the Signs of the Times. The Millennial Reign shall be a time of rest for the people of God.

Sales Price $7.00

Write for other prophetic material.
Richard L. Madison
PO Box 205
Oakman, AL 35579
205 622 3493
205 522 4760

Shipping and Handling $2.00

Cassette Tape List

(See next page for additional tapes)

Cassette Tape Prices	Video Prices
Any single tape - $4.00 each 5 or more tapes - $3.00 each 6 tape prophecy set - $20.00	Any one for $15.00 Any 3 or more for only $12.00 each

---

45 Minute Song Tape by Laura Madison

Look What The Lord Has Done - $7.00

US FUNDS - ONLY
Note: Please add $2.00 for shipping